DUST

Remember Thou Art

SPLENDOR

DUST
Remember Thou Art
SPLENDOR

by the

REVEREND RAOUL PLUS, S.J.

Translated from the French
by
SISTER MARY BERTILLE
and
SISTER MARY ST. THOMAS
SISTERS OF NOTRE DAME
of
CLEVELAND, OHIO

FREDERICK PUSTET CO., (INC.)
Publishers
NEW YORK AND CINCINNATI
1941

Nihil Obstat:

ARTHUR J. SCANLAN, S.T.D.,
Censor Librorum.

Imprimatur:

✠ FRANCIS J. SPELLMAN, D.D.,
Archbishop of New York.

New York, January 23, 1941.

To the Holy Trinity
Whose Divine Indwelling
Makes of Our Dust
True Splendor

FOREWORD

FROM a material standpoint, most of us put forth much effort to live according to our station in life. Not infrequently, however, we strain our energies in feverish and restless exertion, to live according to some worldly standard, which we, in our exaggerated idea of our own importance, conceive to be our appropriate plane of living. Somehow the tendency to overestimate our position far exceeds our inclination to minimize it, even though a humbler opinion of our social status might be more in accord with the promptings of honesty.

By a strange inconsistency we do

7

just the contrary from a spiritual standpoint. We generally set ourselves standards far below those in keeping with the station to which we were born.

On the day of our baptism, we were born to a royal state; but how often we act like men, who though possessing incalculable wealth, persist in living on a pauper's level. The world would consider such conduct abnormal. In the spiritual lives of many of us, however, it is not at all unusual.

Stranger still, not only do we fail to live in keeping with our spiritual wealth, but we very often live utterly oblivious of the fortune that is ours. We would speak with pity of a man who after a frustrated life due to lack of means would discover on his

8

deathbed that throughout his life he had possessed a great fortune of which he never knew. "The irony of fate!" we might exclaim.

Alas, spiritually, how many frustrated lives there are! For none of them can we exclaim, "the irony of fate!" We might more truthfully say, "Oh, the perversity of human nature that would not know!" Yet out of compassion for the tragedy of so many sightless and uncomprehending souls we might more fittingly echo our Savior's sigh of pity: *If they did but know the gift of God.*

This book, then, will reveal to many the *Gift of God.* It seeks to encourage them to capitalize on the tremendous wealth of which they have been so long unaware; to urge them to live

9

always on the highest, noblest plane—
the only one befitting their true position as *co-heirs with Christ*. Here
there is no danger of overevaluating
this position, but rather a perilous
tendency to underestimate its importance.

The age-old motto, *noblesse oblige*,
that kept before the minds of royalty's
children their duty to act on high
principles because of their privileged
birth, finds its spiritual counterpart in
the title of this book. God's children,
too, can never forget that theirs is a
royal sonship; they are more than the
dust of which they are made: *Dust, remember thou art splendor!*

CONTENTS

DUST

Remember Thou Art

SPLENDOR

Chapter I

OUR BAPTISMAL SPLENDOR

KNOWING that, just because we are mortals, we might easily forget our mortality, the Church, on the first day of Lent, signs our foreheads with symbolic ashes: *Remember that, whether you like it or not, thou art dust, and unto dust thou shalt return.*

However opportune such a reminder might be, it is not what I wish to insist upon now. I prefer to stress the marvelous grandeur to which we are all called: *Dust, remember that thou art splendor!*

In this frail envelope of our body is enclosed a great marvel. I am not referring to the marvel of our soul

15

only, but more especially to the life that God designs to live in each of us, if we are, and in so far as we are, in the state of grace.

For such is our destiny: we are not made to be mere human beings but rather to be divinized human beings. Our true description is: "a soul in a body and God in that soul."

* * *

When we entered into human existence on the day of our birth, we had no participation in the divine life— only one creature entered into human existence and divine life at one and the same time: that was the Virgin Mary; we call this privilege the Immaculate Conception.

Neither you nor I had the privilege

16

of *Immaculate Conception*; on the contrary, what poignant truth in the words of the *Miserere*: *In sin did my mother conceive me!* Certainly, she committed no sin in bringing me into the world, this dear holy woman; but on account of original sin, she could transmit to me only a human nature deprived of the gifts which God would have bestowed had the first human couple remained faithful.

Not being immaculate in our conception, or in other words deprived of supernatural grace from our entrance into human existence, we could never see God face to face, never know the joys of heaven.

Ask the table before which you are seated to place an act of intelligence; it is incapable of it. To do it, the nature of the table would have to be enriched with special and miraculous gifts. Consider a human being: It is nothing more than a human being when it comes into existence. Ask it to place a supernatural act; it is incapable of it—incapable, unless a superior force seizes it on the level of its unqualified human nature and transports it to a splendidly elevated plane: the domain of the human divinized. Baptism is that superior force. No other force in our lives, not even our First Holy Communion, approached it in importance.

Had we died as infants without having been marked with the waters of Baptism, we could never possess the Beatific Vision. We would not be punished, of course, but we could

18

enjoy only a natural happiness, proportionate to our own human nature, nothing more; for, not having been elevated to a state higher than nature, we could enjoy nothing beyond that state.

Picture yourself then as you were shortly after your birth—a poor frail being. What were you? A poor little pagan. You were carried to the church and brought to the baptismal font. On the threshold of the church, the priest, in the name of Jesus Christ, asked you: "What dost thou ask of the Church of God?"

Your godfather and your godmother answered for you: "Faith."

"To what doth Faith bring thee?"

"Life everlasting."

The whole object of the baptismal rite is to introduce divine life into your soul. As a result of original sin, the demon obtained the power to deprive you of the possession of God at your entrance into existence. But Baptism strips the demon of this right God permitted him to exercise over you and every other human being entering into the world. And—greater even than this negative consideration—Baptism effects God's entrance into your soul.

Consider the words of the priest: "Go out from this child, unclean spirit, and give place to the Holy Spirit."

Is not that sufficiently clear, sufficiently formal?

Note the expression *this child under*

the momentary power of the unclean spirit—you were that child.

Two or three times in the name of Christ, the priest renewed the injunction: "Go, depart, it is finished! Give place henceforth, unclean spirit, to the Holy Spirit!"

When, some minutes after, the essential rite of Baptism took place: "I baptize thee in the name of the Father, and of the Son, and of the Holy Ghost," the demon saw himself obliged to withdraw from your soul. Then into your regenerated soul entered silently triumphant, the Holy Spirit, or rather the entire Trinity, since the Father and the Word are always equally present with the Holy Spirit.

It is a very beautiful truth, is it

not? It was with good reason surely that Léon Allé-La Prune wrote in his private notes:

"I am a Christian by the grace of God."

"To be a Christian is the gift of God and the greatest of all gifts.

"Do I realize what it means to be a Christian?

"Do I think of it?

"The Christian is, one might say, a deified man. Living the life of grace, I am participating in the divine life itself.

"It is not enough to be a Christian through habit or through sentiment, I wish to be one *in light* and *with reflection*. I wish to think of what I am, to realize it, to sound its depths."

But perhaps you will say: "That's

fine, only I have never been baptised; I am a loyal, honest, and upright soul; but I was born into a family without the faith."

Baptism of water is the normal means to enter into the possession of divine life, but for you who through no fault of your own are deprived of the normal means, baptism of desire, or baptism of blood may effect the same grace.

We will not discuss baptism of blood since it applies to one who, well on the way toward professing the faith, dies for Christ before having been able to receive the baptism of water.

There remains the baptism of desire, namely, the desire of doing in accordance with God's will and through devotion to Him, all that is necessary to be saved. A child, until he has reached the use of reason, must receive baptism of water in order to be raised to the supernatural state. Since he does not yet possess the conscious use of his faculties, he cannot make an act of desire. Consider the case of an adult pagan: If out of respect for the Supreme Being whom he can not but discover as dominating his life and demanding of him moral rectitude, he remains faithful and chooses the good the first time he finds himself face to face with a serious act of which his conscience disapproves, he is by this fact, raised to the supernatural state. There is produced in him then the equivalent of that which takes place normally at the baptism of water.

God enters his soul and if this adult remains faithful thereafter in all grave matters, the divine life remains in him. God gives every soul sufficient opportunity to be saved. According to Saint Thomas Aquinas, God would, if need be, send an angel to a soul in good faith to reveal to him the truths necessary for salvation.

In the case just presented, the adult does not know all these truths explicitly, but if, through hypothesis, he decides to admit and to practice all that is necessary, there is, on his part, implicit adherence to the true faith. If, however, after having been raised by such an act to the supernatural state, the adult in question falls gravely; or, if he discovers or even only suspects with just reason that he is not in the truth, and neglects to enlighten himself, thereby sinning gravely against the light, he loses the divine life which was in him.

Can you, then, who have never received the baptism of water, possess what Catholic doctrine calls the state of grace, namely, that incomparable participation in the life of God granted to the soul the moment it is made a Christian? I answer you very decidedly, *yes*. But I ask you, "How do you live? Can you say that every time you are confronted with an important problem of conscience, you always decide upon the good, not only because of your human desire for moral rectitude, but through devotion to Him whose existence your reason or your religion, or whatever it may

26

be, cannot but affirm? Are you truly loyal? Have you never sinned against the Spirit?

If you can answer these questions affirmatively, do not be sad; the doors to divine life will not be closed to you. The means for you may not be the normal means. Nevertheless, that does not prevent the truth from remaining objectively the truth, the good from remaining objectively what it really is and not what someone thinks it is. Whence follows the duty of each to seek the light, and the duty of the Church to preach the Gospel to the farthest bounds of the earth and to the end of time.

Each one will be judged not on Truth in itself and Good in itself but upon that which he thought *in good faith* to be true and good, and upon the conformity of his conduct to his belief. To belong *in good faith* to error is to belong in the depths of one's soul to the Truth.

But let us suppose that you have been baptised with the baptism of water. In that case, let me ask you, "Do you live in conformity with the demands of your baptism at least in every important matter? Do you observe justice? Do you practice charity? Are you faithful to your duties toward God: to those, at least, which constitute a grave obligation? Do you betray your home in the slightest way? Do you live in honesty and essential purity?"

Ah, then I congratulate you! God lives in your soul. You are a living tabernacle of the Most High; you are a reliquary of the Trinity. Do you doubt such splendor?

Let me endeavor to reveal the full radiance of this splendor.

Chapter II

OUR ORIGINAL DIVINIZATION

WHEN water bubbles up from the earth and a spring issues from the ground, is it not an indication that there is somewhere a subterranean body of water feeding this spring?

On the day of our baptism, the blessed water touched our foreheads and that water together with the sacramental words brought divine life to our souls, consecrating us living tabernacles of the Most High. But whence comes this water? Where is the source of this divine life?

We can trace it back through the

ages by means of the signs left to us. Saint John tells us that, at the foot of the cross, he saw blood and water flowing from the side of the Savior. Ah, that gives us a clue! At the beginning of His public ministry, in the conversation both with the woman of Samaria and with Nicodemus, Our Lord speaks of water which united with the Holy Spirit has the power to make us participators in the divine nature, "water springing forth to eternal life." It is to this height that we must be elevated—to the life of God! Shall we try to ascend there now in spirit?

*   *   *

The life of God consists essentially in God the Father understanding Himself in an act of intelligence of such prodigious value that this very act bursts forth in the state of a subsistent Person, the Word, the Wisdom of the Father, infinite like the One from whom It emanates.

By way of simple comparison, suppose the act of intelligence that you are making now—your act of grasping what I am telling you—emanated not from a limited person, finite and imperfect like yourself, but from someone who has infinity in his essence. Instead of being transitory and deficient this act of understanding would be, because of the nature of the one making it, eternal, infinite, sovereignly perfect. . . .

Of course, I am not offering an explanation, but merely an adumbration of the Trinity.

Now, between this Father and this Word there is a mutual impulse of love arising in the Divinity as another subsistent Person: Love in person, the Holy Spirit.

And that generation proceeds eternally, uniquely, infinitely. . . .

God is all sufficient to Himself!

Yet, one blessed day—the day time was created, for until then there had been only eternity—it pleased God to go out from the infinite solitude of His Being, and to place side by side with His unique Being other beings who would be reflections of Himself. A prodigious mystery! It constitutes one of the most difficult problems that can ever confront human reason.

God, lavish in His gifts, hurled

33

across space—and on that day space was created—planets by the thousands: planets of whose beauty and magnitude you can begin to catch a glimmer when on a beautiful clear night you see some two hundred sixty million stars in the celestial canopy.

We shall not dwell on this thought but continue.

Among these millions of stars of which you perceive only a very few, there is a little planet at once magnificent and insignificant—the earth. Insignificant! What is the earth among the vast multitude of planets? A pinhead is hardly perceptible in the room you now occupy, and the earth in the immensity of creation is less than that!

It is, nevertheless, a magnificent

34

planet! The great geologist George Termier, in his beautiful book *A la Gloire de la Terre*, describes how it took some thousands of years for our earth to become what it is today. God prepared for His creatures a magnificent dwelling place. As a mother plans long in advance and with great love the hope chest she wishes to give her child, so God bending over our planet thought of us while preparing the beautiful gift He was to give the first human couple in Humanity's first marriage.

There is a prodigy more extraordinary still! God communicates to man something of His own life. Through natural creation, He gives us our being. Over and above that, He makes us supernatural, greater than nature: He draws from the immensity of His own wealth, allowing us to participate, in so far as a finite being is able, in the Infinite.

We shall remain, of course, poor, limited, and weak beings, yet beautiful because of our intelligence and liberty. He does even more: He decides to make us His children, and to admit us to His royal intimacy. Our essential vocation consists not in being mere creatures of God, but children of God: *filios Dei fieri* we hear at the last Gospel of the Mass.

Why, alas, must it be that humanity deplorably disdains this divine life thus generously bestowed by God?

Perhaps at this point, the classical objection against original sin suggests itself to you: Why did God wish to make the preservation of the divine in humanity dependent upon a free act of His creature? Why above all did He so will when He foresaw that this free act would be disobedience with resultant loss of supernatural life, not only for Adam and Eve, but for entire humanity?

Without attempting to treat this problem thoroughly, I shall suggest one or two reflections which I think will allay your worries, and not only justify God's way, if that be necessary, but also throw light on the reasonableness of His plan.

In submitting His free and reasonable creature to a trial, God did not violate justice in the least. He owed man nothing; all was grace, a pure gift. Anyone who gives a present can attach whatever conditions he wishes to the obtaining of the gift. Furthermore, do not forget the immeasurable distance between the infinite God and the finite creature.

But has not God failed in goodness?

Let us reflect. Suppose you gave one of your children a bicycle, a rifle, or an auto. Your child by culpable imprudence and wilful disobedience wounds himself with the present that you gave him. Your gift is, nevertheless, a real gift, isn't it?

There is much more to be said than that. In making the preservation of divine life dependent upon man's free will, God doubled His gift with a singular delicacy. His manner of

38

proceeding was more worthy of Himself and of us.

More worthy of us: God exacts an obligatory homage of irrational beings. Stars, light, and rocks, cannot but render glory to God; they simply cannot evade rendering this homage. Almighty God, having bestowed on us intelligence and liberty among our most beautiful natural gifts, recognizes the dignity of our being in asking us to use these splendid advantages for our own supernatural good. What could be more conformable to our dignity?

More worthy of Himself: Assuredly God could have imposed the supernatural state upon us instead of proposing it to us as a recompense of

39

free homage. That would have been less delicate. Think of the infinite distance between the Lord and us! Here is an immensely rich benefactor; he desires to bestow upon an extremely poor person a gift of rare value. If he gives it to him without asking anything in exchange, the recipient will be hurt, because this would only make him feel more keenly the distance between them.

Suppose, on the contrary, that the benefactor expresses himself thus: "Listen, do me this favor, give me this pleasure; I shall return you like for like." Does this not create a sort of bridge between the two, and for the recipient the touching delusion that he has, at least to some extent, merited the gift he is to receive, although in reality, it is entirely gratuitous? Because God has been extremely delicate, let us not reproach Him now as if He were responsible for our presumptuous indifference! A little thoughtful reflection convinces us that the original trial was neither caprice, nor a malicious trick, but one more grace added to grace itself.

Then—and this is the essential answer to the difficulty—God only permitted original sin, because He knew that He Himself would restore the supernatural so deplorably lost, and reinstate our souls in grace according to an order of Providence incomparably more beautiful than the initial order.

In all that we have already said, there has been no question of Christ.

In order to redivinize us God sends His own Son: *God so loved the world*, as Saint Paul said, *that He gave His only Begotten Son.* If there had been no Fall, there would not have been at the climax of the story, Jesus Christ, the Savior.

Forget all you know for a moment.

It is a certain December twenty-fifth in the history of the world. You are, I am supposing, a contemporary of Mary and of the carpenter Joseph. It is about thirty-nine years after the conquest of Judea by the Romans. You live in Palestine in a village called Bethlehem. Someone approaches you early in the morning, "Do you know the news?"

"No."

"Ah, come with me, come out of the village. You see that shelter for animals over there in the fields?"

"Yes."

"Well, if you go there, you will find the Son of God lying on straw in one of the mangers."

"What, the Son of God? Are you joking? The Son of God, I know who He is: He is the Infinite Wisdom of the Father. You are not going to make me believe that it is infinitely wise for the Son of God to come into the world, into a manger meant for animals. . . . You will have to tell that to someone else! I don't believe it!"

"Say what you please! It *is* the Son of God. Besides, go over there; go very near; lean over this strange

43

cradle. Ask the Infant who is there. He Himself will tell you. . . ."

"What, Lord, then it is you? But what are You doing here? What is the reason for such a coming—and in such surroundings?"

"You ask Me what I am doing here. You are right in thinking that it is not this place that has attracted Me. I dreamed together with the Father and the Holy Spirit of inhabiting the living crib of your heart, and because you have refused that joy to Us, you see Me here. . . . You . . . begin to understand?"

Some thirty years pass. You see attached to a gibbet, between two robbers, the Crucified; He is hanging upon those two beams which stand out

44

against the horizon of history. Who is it? Listen! Didn't you just hear the captain of the guard?

"Ah, there is no mistake, this was indeed the Son of God!"

"The Son of God? What are you saying, Centurion? That is a frightful blasphemy. The Son of God there between those two wretches! You can't mean that!"

"Say what you will, but it *is* the Son of God."

"What, Lord, is it You? But why? Why?"

"Ah, you ask Me why? To give back to your soul divine life; for that, for nothing but that. I have paid dearly for your soul's life, you know! Yes, I did this for you. Do you remember some months ago at the

45

well of Jacob, when I spoke to the Samaritan woman, I said to her: 'My poor child, if you knew! If you knew as I know . . . of divine matters; I have full knowledge. The Crib is past for Me; before Me looms the Cross. All this, I suffer for you, for the divine life that is in you. . . . Try then to grasp the full import of this gift of God. The gift of God is God Himself, given to your soul! Look at what it cost Me to restore to your soul this *gift of God*. I beg you, seek to know, to understand, to penetrate its meaning!' "

To know: That is the most profound word of the Gospel. . . . I leave you to ponder over it.

It is of utmost importance that we

46

know, isn't it? Should we have cost so dearly and know nothing about it? Ah! We must know! We want to know!

Chapter III

THE CALL TO BRAVERY

IN speaking of bravery someone said: "It seems to me that life is no longer a problem for one who has discovered what ought to hold first place."

René Schwob wrote similarly: "I think the religion of Christ appears in all its grandeur only in the lives of its heroes for whom the invisible world is everything; it is from their true understanding of the religion of Christ that they draw this dominating motivation which makes their lives heroic."

48

This last thought recalls an old saying which will launch us at once on the subject: "The heroic state is the state of grace!" To keep the divine life received in Baptism, we must exercise no ordinary degree of courage but a valor comparable to or even surpassing the heroism displayed on the fields of battle.

Is our divine life, then, in any danger? Yes, a twofold danger: one coming from the devil, the other from ourselves.

To hold out against these dangers we must practice the highest virtue.

*　　*　　*

There are many who wish to disregard the demon, but they make a mistake. We know from the teaching of the Church that just as God put mankind to a test so too He tried the angels. In what their test consisted, we do not know. Some think that the Most High may have given them a pre-vision of the Holy Humanity of Christ and that they, endowed with an angelic nature, refused to bow down before a God manifesting Himself as a man. Whatever it may have been, this fact is certain: Some of the angels remained faithful and others revolted. The devil was the chief of the traitorous angels. For him and his companions hell was created.

Being powerless to do anything to God, the devil strives, through vengeance, to bring the creatures of God to perdition. By making Adam and Eve fall into sin he succeeded in depriving of the life of supernatural grace each human being who comes into the world. Baptism, however, despoils him of all his rights over the soul. When he hears himself sternly commanded two or three times, "Leave this child, unclean spirit, give place to the Holy Spirit," he is *forced* to leave the human soul.

Do you think he promises not to return? All we know of the devil compels us to think that, on the contrary, he will try the impossible, to return in triumph to the living city from which he has been ejected. The liturgy describes him to us, according to the Scriptures, as prowling about among souls seeking an opening: *circuit quaerens quem devoret*. Of course, he will not show himself in the outfit of a devil, for who then would not answer him as Christ did: "Get thee behind me, Satan! Away, wretch!" He camouflages his game. His pet trick consists in lulling souls into a state of weakness, habituating them to easy living, taking from them the taste for daring, and the energy to do the hard things. This supine life is what the Savior meant by *the world*. It is not sin; it is rather the inaptitude for every hardship; the horror of all that is mortifying, generous, nobly exacting. And that is why Our Lord cursed it. Its spirit is the normal preparation for every cowardice. A serious temptation comes and the soul gives way. Unaccustomed to maintain a firm balance the soul is brought down by the first snare cleverly laid in its path.

The Call to Bravery

Sometimes those who work with young people are perturbed that so many succumb at this age when temptations are severe. They seemed excellent children. Ah, yes, they were! But that is all they were. . . . They had not been trained or at least not sufficiently taught *to will*. At the first attack or after feeble resistance they are overcome and surrender. Psichari used to say: "Conquer yourself by violence." They, on the contrary, let themselves go. "I am not doing anything wrong," they argue. No, perhaps not, but they are creating the exact temperament to succumb when a dangerous allurement entices them. Think then, you who read this, of your first mortal sin, if ever you have had the misfortune of committing one.

Did it take a great deal to make you fall? Now think of what goes on around you daily.

Ah, yes, picture the triumphs of the demon. See this young man, this beautiful young girl, this wife, this married man: They persevered for long in the observance of the baptismal injunction, "Receive this white garment. Carry it without spot to the tribunal of God." Without spot! Alas! They are now no longer without spot! They did not wish to refuse themselves any reading, any flirtation, any imprudence; they denied themselves nothing; they made no effort whatsoever to test out their self-control. They frittered away their time, putting far from them every restraint.

54

Naturally the inevitable happened. There, on the once spotless purity of their baptismal robe, don't you see it —the ugly stain of sin?

How the demon exults as he encamps before the Lord: "Ah! Look at me! I did not have myself crucified for them. And look! I enter as triumphant conqueror into these souls for whom You have given all Your Blood. I have broken the tabernacles or rather they have opened them for me. Who is the stronger of the two, You or I?"

Ah! If it were only true that the sole peril, the principal danger comes from the devil. But no, there are *in us* forces of treason. To gain a better understanding of them let us compare the situation of Adam and Eve on leaving the hands of God and our situation since Christ redeemed us.

God had bestowed on Adam and Eve besides their human nature two types of gifts: the supernatural, namely, that participation in the divine life of which we have spoken; and, in addition, preternatural gifts: the triple faculty of never having to suffer, to die, or to endure the interior revolt of the lower powers—the imagination and the senses—against the superior power—reason enlightened by faith. Let us pass over the exemption from suffering and death to consider here the exemption from evil concupiscence.

After the fall, the supernatural and preternatural gifts were taken

56

away. . . . Then Christ came! He came to restore divine life, that is to say, God's supernatural gifts. He did not choose to give back the preternatural gifts; therefore, we will suffer and die. But that does not interest us now. What does claim our attention is that we shall have to submit to the assaults of evil concupiscence to such an extent that, to quote Pascal, "We shall be as if torn between two infinities." Something in us impels us toward the Most High; we are made for divine life. Something in us draws us to what is lowest; we must live divine life in a degenerate world.

That explains how the power of elevation and the germ of degradation are present at one and the same time in each of us as in all humanity:

in every soul there is the making of
a Father Foucauld or a Marat;[1] the
inclinations of a Thérèse of the Child
Jesus, a Francis Xavier, or tendencies
that make a criminal's end an ever-
present possibility; inspirations to
aim high and enticements to evil alike
flash invitingly before us.

Ah! the ideologies of a Rousseau:
"Man is born good." How little they
are worth if they are taken to mean
that man has only powers for good!
Oh! No! Assuredly man was good on
leaving the hands of God, but original
sin has unbridled in all the instincts
for evil. What folly to appear not to
know that and to conceive of a world
system, notably a doctrine of educa-
tion, without taking into account this

[1] Marat: a reactionary of the French Revolution.

essential factor! Even when one makes an effort to remain faithful in everything do not the dramatic allurements of sin hold powerful attraction? Each can confirm this. Is it not true that at certain times you have felt surge within you desires that could scarcely be called holy? If you had been master of the situation in such and such a circumstance; if the execution of your designs had not been prevented by the presence of a group or the nature of the occasion; if grace, above all, had not come to your assistance; is it not true that there would no longer be a great difference between you and a vile wretch?

You have probably read the words of Gradere to Matilde in Mauriac's *Les Anges Noirs:* "Do you believe that there exist no other crimes than those recorded by the newspapers? Do you know the number of unpunished murderers? I know. There are infinitely more fish in the sea than in the fish-trap or in the nets of the police. You do not know the myriads that wriggle about beyond reach in the great depths."

What a subject for reflection for the many who have never been called before the courts but whose record on judgment day will be far from spotless. Picture the world of sinister apparitions that will emerge from apparently honest consciences on that day of decisive revelations, that moment when true history will begin. "I do not know what the conscience of a rascal is, I only know my own. It is

not very beautiful!" said Joseph de
Maistre.

How could we fail then to see eye
to eye with the Church's insistence on
the necessity of prudence for the practice of virtue? When we considered
the tactics of the devil we felt how reasonable is a generous firmness. Do
we not discover here the imperious necessity of the first of the cardinal vir-
tues? Since we each have within us
the power of treason, we must be on
our guard not to run risks presump-
tuously. He who exposes himself to
danger will perish in it. But what is
more evident than the moral bank-
ruptcy of our times with respect to the
virtue of prudence.

Pharisaical we should not be, but
with the Church and a well-defined

61

moral law we ought to hold in horror
the fretful worry of those who see sin
in everything, everywhere! There is
a vast difference, however, between
seeing an occasion of sin in everything
and seeing no sin in anything.

Confidence certainly! Divine help
is always with us; we ought to trust
in the merits of the Cross of Christ!
Still we must be on the alert not to
expose ourselves to temptation. God
helps those who help themselves. It
is folly to suppose that we will emerge
uncontaminated from the occasion of
sin after throwing ourselves headlong
into it with gaiety of heart.

Is it too much to ask you to examine
your conscience honestly? One fights
well when convinced of the purpose
of his warfare. You are each—man

or woman—possessors of an incomparable treasure. This treasure, as Holy Scripture says, you carry in *earthen vessels*.

Have you the necessary courage to keep it intact?

Have you the prudence not to expose it?

It remains for you in the secret of your conscience to question yourself before God, to answer loyally, and, if need be, to act.

CHAPTER IV

THE CALL TO INTIMACY

HOW many times have we not heard Christian souls express the longing to live in intimacy with God, to have with Him more than simple, formal and semi-official relations limited to occasional acts of devotion observed more to fulfill a command than to respond to a real need of love!

Often one asks: "What can I do to attain to this intimacy?" "What is the basis of a life of true union with God?"

Blessed are you if you desire divine intimacy! No grace could be more precious for you than this yearning to leave off formalism in order to live intensely our magnificent religion.

* * *

If you have followed the preceding chapters, you certainly must have discovered the help given for divine intimacy by the marvelous Presence that entered your soul at Baptism. Let us consider it more closely.

Never to drive God from one's soul is an essential but a negative task. The true Christian will wish to do more. Having sounded the depths of the gift of God, he sees that it consists not only in the presence of a certain *something* in his soul, and in the super-elevation of his powers of knowing and loving, but in the intimate presence of *Someone*, the Great Someone, of the Holy Trinity Itself. From this conviction he will advance to the realization that the logic of love requires him to cultivate this Divine Presence, to honor It, to make the most of It, to surround It with a positive devotion.

Do we not keep a lamp burning constantly before the Blessed Sacrament? Should not a light watch constantly in our own hearts before God who through love dwells there as long as we have the happiness of being in the state of grace? "Let us enter into our own heart," said Father Judde, an author of the seventeenth century, "let us listen and obey." He added, "Let more than half of yourself be always there, attentive to what is said there,

66

to what goes on there, and I will answer for your perfection."

If among the best Christians many lack an interior spirit, it is because they do not sufficiently fathom the mystery of the Divine Indwelling. They lack faith and motivation.

They lack faith. Recall what we said of Baptism: The day we received the sacrament of birth to Christian life, we were consecrated living tabernacles of the Holy Trinity. Does not the word *tabernacle* evoke the parallel between the presence of God in our soul through the state of grace received at Baptism and the presence of our Lord in our hearts as a result of Holy Communion?

A practical and extremely harmful error exists among many Christians, perhaps even among you who read these lines. Were I to ask you what you mean by the Real Presence, you would probably answer immediately: "The Eucharistic Presence." Yes, certainly that is a magnificent Real Presence! But is the Eucharist the only sacrament of the Real Presence?

What do you consider Baptism to be? Why do you say that there is a Real Presence at the Consecration of the Mass when the priest changes bread into the Body of Christ and wine into His Blood, and only a metaphorical Presence at Baptism when the priest bending over the infant at the baptismal font makes the Holy Spirit enter into him with the words, "Give place to the Holy Spirit." No, indeed, the Eucharist and Baptism are

68

both sacraments of the Real Presence. In both instances the Presence is actual, even though, as you clearly see, the mode of the Presence differs.

Who then becomes present at Baptism? The Three Divine Persons. The Holy Spirit especially is named; but we know that where one of the Divine Persons is present the other two are always equally present. The single exception is in the case of the Incarnation where only the Second Person took a human body in the womb of the Blessed Virgin Mary.

Who is present in the Eucharist? Jesus the God-Man, He who once lived in Palestine continues now His human-divine presence in the tabernacles of our altars.

Through the sacrament of Baptism,

69

the Three Divine Persons are present with a presence of spirit—somewhat as our soul is present in our body. Through the sacrament of the Eucharist, Jesus, the Word Incarnate, is present with the body that Mary gave Him. Baptism and the Eucharist: two sacraments of the Real Presence. The resemblances between these two sacraments are more striking than the differences; their effects are practically the same—God in us in either case. Then, why not treat the spiritual Presence of God in us through Baptism in a manner analogous to that in which we regard the physical Presence of Jesus in the tabernacles of our churches?

A missionary relates this story: Because a certain priest could visit one of his missions only at long intervals, he had refused to let the Blessed Sacrament in the chapel. The faithful promised that if they were permitted to have the Eucharistic Presence, they would never leave Our Lord alone and that they would delegate someone to watch and to pray constantly before Jesus enclosed in the tabernacle. . . . What a lesson these neophytes give us Christians born in the faith! We shall not speak here of the little we do for the Eucharistic Presence. Let us consider rather what we do for the Baptismal Presence.

What man or woman thinks daily of entering into the depths of his soul to find God there and to render Him loving, living homage?

There are twenty-four hours or

fourteen hundred forty minutes in one day. How many of them do we use to come to greet God who dwells within us intimately if we are in the state of grace, as I well suppose we are. How appallingly thoughtless we are! All day long, if we wish—since our state of grace depends upon our will —we are ciboria of the Trinity. We do not even bother ourselves about it. It doesn't mean a thing to us.

"How many souls," writes Monsignor d'Hulst, "How many souls will utter one day a cry of amazement to discover the marvelous reality they carried within them without ever knowing it!"

Without doubt, union with God is above all else a union of the will with God consisting essentially in devotion to the duty of one's state. How much the relatively frequent thought of God would facilitate this union.

Why should I not urge you strongly to these frequent withdrawals into your own heart since they are so fruitful for the spiritual life and prepare the soul for the most precious interior graces God may wish to give? Let your Christianity be more than simple formalism; aspire to live within! Learn to dwell in your own soul. It is worth the effort I assure you. If you but knew how great it is! If you only knew! . . .

Marie Antoinette de Geuser, who died at the age of twenty-nine, was the eldest of twelve children of whom nine were boys. Her mother's prolonged illness often obliged her to take complete charge of the home. In spite of her many duties she could make this resolution: "I will be the little one occupied with the *Great Forgotten One.*"

She understood *the great secret* as did Elizabeth of the Trinity, another daughter of our day, who became a Carmelite at Dijon. Elizabeth, whose life story is a true inspiration as well as a fascinating biography, used to say: "I have found heaven on earth, since heaven is God and I have God in my soul."

Is not that what Saint Augustine said? After having long sought God everywhere but in the depths of his own heart, the learned doctor discovered through the study of the dogma of sanctifying grace the great

Reality of realities: God deigning to live His life in the depths of the soul. From then on, Saint Augustine affirms, he never sought elsewhere the basis for his intimacy with the Most High. *Deus intimo meo intimior*, he exulted: "God is closer to me than I to myself."

Were not Saint Teresa and Father Foucauld equally penetrated with this tremendous truth? Saint Teresa wrote in the thirteenth chapter of *The Way of Perfection*: "Think that there is within you a magnificent palace. If you endeavored to remember that you possess in your soul a guest of such majesty, you would not be able, I am sure, to become engrossed, as you do, in the things of earth. If I had known formerly, as I know now, that a great King dwells in this little palace of my soul, it seems to me that I would not have left Him alone so often."

The holy hermit of Hoggar Father Charles Foucauld in a letter to his sister, the mother of a family, gave these precious counsels: "God is in you, in the depths of your soul, always, always there listening to you and asking you to speak a little with Him. . . .

"Accustom your children to speak with the divine Guest of their soul; remind them often that for us Christians there is no solitude—God is within us.

"This is, as far as my weakness permits, my very life, my dear. Try to make it more your own; it will not isolate you, nor keep you from your other occupations; it takes only a minute, and instead of your being alone there will be two to fulfill your duties. From time to time look into your heart, recollect yourself for a quarter of a minute and say: 'You are there, my God, I love You.' It will not take you any longer than that, and all that you do will be better because you have help. . . . Little by little you will acquire the habit of recollection, and finally you will feel constantly the presence of this sweet Companion, the God of our hearts. Let us pray for one another that we may be lovingly attentive to this dear Guest of our souls."

Who would refuse to heed this counsel? Father Foucauld is addressing a person in the world. You live in the world; this counsel is for you.

God grant you an understanding of His Presence, and the desire as well as the courage to make It the impelling force of your life.

CHAPTER V

THE CALL TO JOY

IS it not irony and a most daring paradox to speak of joy in the trying times through which we are now passing? No, in the midst of her preparations for the mysteries of Holy Week, the Church consecrates one Sunday, Laetare Sunday, to joy. Like the Church, we too rejoice in our sorrow. Not that we forget the Cross; for the Cross does not allow itself to be forgotten. But to increase our courage in the face of the existing or threatening trials, what could be more fruitful or beneficial than to meditate

79

upon the profound reasons we have for maintaining our interior peace amid the tribulations of this valley of tears?

*   *   *

As has already been said: God does not will us to be mere human beings. He made us partakers of His divine nature. This supplementary and supernatural life, this life transcending natural life, which was lost by the disobedience of Adam, is the life Christ came to restore to us through the Crib, His thirty-three years of life with us, and the Cross. . . .

Before returning to His Father, the Savior instituted Baptism first among the Sacraments that we might be born to the divine life at our very entrance into existence. The day the baptismal water touched our foreheads, we became living ciboria of the Most High, tabernacles of the Trinity. *Dust, remember thou art splendor!* If we are now without mortal sin God dwells in our very being, giving eternal value to every part and parcel of our existence.

Many have left their loved ones to go to the army, others for the sake of defense or safety have had to evacuate their homes. Many at this very moment are enduring intense anguish. What a source of peace, if we live in Christian fidelity, to be able to say, wherever we may be, whatever may be our age or condition of existence: "God dwells in my soul; in joy and in sorrow He is with me; we are always two, He and I. I am a living Cathedral whose exterior, bombs and shells, accident or illness may strike, but whose interior can never be deprived of its Real Presence."

The Christian does not belittle the human joys that God permits him: health, every passing day, the radiance of the sun which inspired the beautiful canticle of St. Francis of Assisi, loyal friends, and the joys of family life. If you have read *Etapes de ma vie* by René Bazin you are familiar with these lines addressed to our Lord:

THANKSGIVING FOR LIFE!

I thank thee, O God, for the colors I have enjoyed, for the diversity of form . . . and for this newness Thou hast put for us in familiar things. . . .

82

> *I thank Thee for deep affections and enduring friendships. . . .*
> *I thank Thee for each year's flowers in my garden and in the fields.*

These beautiful human joys, however, are not the only joys. The main reason for the joy of the Christian in the state of grace is the intimate possession of God within him. *I bring you tidings of great joy*—incomparable happiness, the Angels sang over the crib of the Most High. The Savior did not come to inhabit the humble stable. He came to restore to men the divine life lost by Adam. The whole Gospel is summed up in that thought. We know, don't we, what is meant by good tidings? As

St. Augustine says so admirably in one of those succinct formulas of which he holds the secret: *Habetis patrem*, you have a Father, God has made you His son. *Habetis patriam*, heaven is your home. *Habetis patrimonium*, you have found your heritage, that is, sanctifying grace which is divine life through participation —divine life possessed in its germ here below and destined to develop to completeness in heaven.

In the possession of this three-fold treasure which is one reality under a triple light: A divine Father to cherish us, a divine homeland to receive us, a Guest thrice holy to dwell within our soul, do we not have all that we need to make us happy?

A soul in grace can truly say: "The miseries of earth may encompass me; suffering, illness, separations, mourning may assail me; war may sound its roar of shells and destruction, but I possess deep interior joy. Suppose, even, that I am deprived of everything, still nothing is wanting to me; I can say with Saint Paul cast into prison: *I exceedingly abound with joy in the midst of tribulations.* "Since I possess within me substantial charity, that is to say, since God lives in me and shares my solitude and misery, I am neither alone nor unhappy; I am unspeakably happy, superabounding in joy." Father Olivaint, martyr of the Commune of 1871, while in the prison of Roquette, gave expression to this same conviction, as did the hermit of the Sahara Father Charles Foucauld in his solitude of Hoggar.

The Apostle Paul, Father Olivaint, and Father Foucauld had faith; that explains their joy.

They knew! They knew the gift of God, but not as we, with a superficial, vapid knowledge that is powerless to grasp its object, to comprehend its full import. God living in them was a *reality*. A reality to which all the powers of their souls clung, a living, existing, throbbing something which was the only thing that counted. What did I say, something? The great *Someone*, the *only Someone*.

Having Him, what mattered all they lacked? "They may take away my liberty, my health, my life," Saint

Paul cries from the depth of his prison, "but they cannot take away love, they cannot take away God who lives in me. In prison? No, I am not in prison, I am in heaven, I tell you, I superabound in joy!"

Fanaticism, you will think. The vocabulary of an emotional, romantic individual. Words, nothing but words.

Ah, no! To be exact, it is we who live in the unreal. If enthusiasm for soaring above our valley of tears is wanting to us, it is because we have forgotten our Baptism and the splendors it brought with it. It is not the Apostle Paul who is deceived and inflamed beyond reason. It is we who lack reason in not knowing how to be inflamed.

87

The time has come to believe in our splendors. While the ornate setting of world prosperity remained standing there was danger of its screening from us the invisible realities we hold within; but now the ornate setting is crumbling . . . it is about to fall . . . it is falling. Its fall will be of an immense service to us if we wake up suddenly and definitely to the essential.

Certainly, I pray as you that earth may be kind to us. But for mercy sake, don't forget the heaven that is in you. . . . May human happiness continue to smile on you; but if it withdraws bit by bit, look within you. God dwells there. God in your soul, is that nothing?

It is everything.

And precisely because it is the unique *all*, the only reality whose absence plunges us into true misfortune; the only reality whose presence gives us essential happiness, the Church, on the day of our baptism, recommended to us joyous living: *Serve the Lord in joy.* Be always in the state of grace; in other words, live always as one baptised, faithful to your baptism, and you will retain forever, come what may, the possession of holy joy.

"Joy," said Chesterton, "is the gigantic secret of the Christian."

Ah! let us keep our gigantic secret!

The war which gives to some the occasion of very great sacrifices necessarily brings to all and will bring to all many occasions of annoyance. Accept them with a smile, with the smile of a soul in peace with God.

The little motto *Keep Smiling* which used to be posted in the New York subways and other such busy places was a discreet invitation to the hurrying, jostling crowds to keep patient.

Let us offer the little and great annoyances of present day existence with a view to obtaining great blessings for the immense interests which are at stake. The manner in which one gives is worth much more than what one gives. Keep smiling!

And whatever may be the height to which the "waters of tribulation rise" let us always elevate our souls higher like those aquatic plants which never let themselves become submerged by the tide, but lift their stems to display their invincible and smiling flowers above the surface of the current.